Icarus Still Flies

I0117672

Nigel Pearce

chipmunkapublishing
the mental health publisher

Published by
Chipmunkapublishing
PO Box 6872
Brentwood
Essex CM13 1ZT
United Kingdom

http://www.chipmunkapublishing.com

Copyright © Nigel Pearce 2011

Edited by Martine Daniel

Chipmunkapublishing gratefully acknowledge the support of Arts Council England.

Author Biography

He was born in 1959. Home was troubled a troubled place to be, exacerbated by profound philosophical disagreements. Consequently he ran away to London age 13 where he lived in the 'counter-culture'. Became ill was then placed in the in the Care of the local council. Fostered to a radical academic couple, although that didn't survive long and he went back underground; eventually being arrested in Guildford. At 14 he went to live in Hollymoor Hospital in Birmingham; this would be age 14-16.He was fairly frequently restrained and given injections of chlorpromazine. Lived for a short time in the 'Birmingham Settlement', but became ill again and was moved to a specialist manic-depressive unit where he first had ECT, age 16. Substance abuse continued with regularly admissions to Central Hospital with psychotic episodes and would sometimes go into semi-catatonic states for periods. At 20 he was diagnosed with schizophrenia.

Some of the admissions were for periods of around a year. At the age 25 had specialist help with substance abuse problems and he has been 'clean' 25 years and 'dry 13 years'. In 1984 he spent a year in Central Hospital, two years in a Pre-discharge Unit in the community and then eight years in 'group homes', but he now lives in his own flat. His body became toxic with medication in 2003 and was seriously ill physically. During the whole period there have been always been some nurses etc who have made his life difficult because of his firmly held leftist ideological perspective. However there were left-wing nurses and social workers who, particularly in the 1970' and early 1980's, behaved in an exception way. He gained a BA (Hons) at the Open University in 1999, 'Certificate in English Studies' at Warwick University in 2007 and is working for a 'Diploma in Creative Writing and Literature' at the Open University at present. Enjoys working in an Oxfam Bookshop once a week and runs a small 'outsider' magazine.

Let me introduce you to this collection of poetry and studies and elucidate the origins and nature of my love of writing and ideas. How writing and reading are essential and, ironically, contributed to my entry into the psychiatric system in 1974 just before my 14 birthday, but have sustained throughout.

Books and ideas were both an early love and haven in a troubled family. Aged 12 I met an English teacher who introduced me to new poetry and then a radical lecturer and some of his students, we debated many concepts and writing generally; the relationship between writing and ideas.

The increasing involvement with the crowd at the university made the fault lines at home particularly sharp. I lived in a bubble of revolutionaries, a few writers, a couple of artists and many people who had simply renounced a conventional way of life; it suited me. I went to live in an avant-garde squat in London and was introduced to 'experimental art' such as 'happenings'.

Poetry, radical ideas and everyday life simply merged into a dream. Within a year I was in a psychiatric unit being restrained and injected with Largactal. Two years later, aged 16, Ihad enforced ECT. I have never stopped reading and writing and have a B.A. (Hons) from the Open University, certificate in English Studies from Warwick University and am now studying for a Diploma in Creative Writing and Literature back at the O.U. Possibly most importantly meet others who believe in the transformative power of writing and thinking as I always will.

Nigel Pearce

Introduction to Experimental Poems No 1-6

Poetry, "stream of consciousness" writing and 'Beat' culture spontaneity.

This introduction examines the historical and theoretical context in which these Experimental Poems: No 1-6 were written.

A method of writing which was developed with Freud's theory of the unconscious became known as "stream of consciousness". It was an attempt to penetrate into the great subterranean ocean of the unconscious. This writing was characterized by an inner monologue which was:

> *"The direct introduction into the interior life of the character."*~ Edouard Dujurdin.

Hence the reader would, by a free flow of language, gain access to the unconscious world. James Joyce and Virginia Woolf are examples of 20th century writers who combined "stream of consciousness" techniques with realism. They wove complex patterns of language which were inspired, to a considerable extent, by Freud's discoveries regarding the nature of the psyche. The relationship between ego and id was of particular interest to those who would explore the mind for the raw material of literature.

Like all "stream of consciousness" writing, these poems are an attempt to "tune into" twilight areas of awareness which are inaccessible through conventional forms and, therefore, to illuminate the id, the unconscious.

In an essay written by Allen Ginsberg, a 'Beat' poet entitled: 'Abstraction in Poetry' (1959) he suggests that the poet:

> *"Reduces the artistic medium to it'sessential*
> *properties."*
> ~ Allen Ginsberg.

This could, he argued, be the poetry of "pure sound" (Ginsberg) like some of the Dadaist poets. However, for Ginsberg, writers such as William S. Burroughs created an abstraction not merely of "pure sound" but, also, with the energy of an "altered state of awareness", the vibrant condition of "pure mind" (Ginsberg). Their work exhibited the negation of a consciousness which is enslaved to the perceptions of the ego:

> *"The sensation of self-elimination ofall being into*
> *the unconscious is theexperience of pure poetry."*
> ~Allen Ginsberg.

In his 1959 essay, mentioned above, Ginsberg describes William S.Burroughs' writing as:

> *"a noncommittal transcript into words of a*
> *succession of visual images passing in front of his*
> *mental eye."*
> ~ Allen Ginsberg.

However, the most significant aspect of writing, for the 'Beat' authors, was not their opiate induced dreaming, but the technique of spontaneous expression which was inspired by listening to improvised jazz:

> *"to sketch the flow that already exists intact in the*
> *mind."*
> ~ Jack Kerouac.

So, in conclusion, these poems are an attempt to transcend ego awareness and swim in a sea of unconsciousness by employing the techniques of experimental poetry to open the doors of perception.

Experimental poem: number 1

Caressed
the echo of a void
embraces reverberation,

Ache
descends in a river
breaking the clasp of mind.

We are engulfed in this swimming of the id
being tuned for a birthing of primal mother,
She wept with the stroking of acid droplets
those have been caught in a leaking chalice.

These eyes are dissolved with a flickering
of colours that is a still pool in the twilight.

Experimental poem: number 2

Poetry
lives in a crystal
teardrop,

It
is here that worms
burrow

Spewing
like the earth retching
lava,

Clasped
by the mind manacles
slicing

the body into daylight and the darkness,
night is whispering with her misty breath.

Experimental poem: number 3

Sand
just flows
through a honeycomb mind,

Ideas
are blown
across an iridescent wasteland

dissolving into an ocean of beats,
we throb, a pulse with this blood

wept
in eyes
cried for wandering poetry,

Descend
into swarms
of crawling echoes

like the dissonant rhythm of chaos.

Experimental poem: number 4

Tied
to a stake,
this ravishing of fire

caresses
the free thought
of the shrouded solitary mind,

Heretics
burn in their emancipation,
the purity of our conflagration

Caresses
the cruel laughter
of a celebrant who is mocking

us, we sing in the finitude of our damnation,
visionaries, we are incarcerated in the flames.

Experimental poem: number 5

White light
licks into an abyss
with the touch of totality,

the
tongue draws a kiss
murmuring with redolence,

this is eternity with whispered dew,
begin our sobbing like a dried lake,
the butterfly is caught in morning flight

wrapped in a veil, his temple of mediocrity,
she is beginning to scribe oceans of lemon,
here night and its burning tears are coaxed

into humming, the drowsiness is like twilight.

Experimental poem: number 6

The lunar
chasm of verse
free with association,

ivy acid
dissolving the page
into running plagues of

caged rats,
wire trap-door is
opening onto the desert

as masks are cast in rivers of clay,
the smile of a bemused mystic at night,
she is writing with those caustic tears of fire

to be entranced in the cloudy liquid of dreams,
spike is eased into the mainline as infinity beckons.

She said: 'love is not enough'

Stole
a ticket
to her theatre

Danced
with this
ballerina of hurricanes.

Dropped
words into
her bronze head

That
sparked, enflamed
and revolutionized us.

Her
nails dug
into taut skin

Leaving
rivulets of
tingling red liquid

Which
flowed into
my bamboo pen.

I
wrote lines
of love welcoming

Her
lunar landscape,
Here we wandered

With
Molotov cocktails
primed and ready

For
encounters with
fascists or renegades.

But she became a reactionary, interrogating
consciousness, examining my arms like a drug-squad
officer.

She said: 'You've got a needle-mark... a needle-mark
from last night.'
I replied: 'That was the only opportunity to visit my
friends, the only chance to get away from your tight
tangle. Yes there is a needle mark, we shoot bliss it's
called white light white heat.'

So
lost in
wastelands of ice.

Here
is where
poets and artists

Freeze
their colours
into brittle webs

Of
nerves and
then sever them.

The

Icarus Still Flies

tragedy
is acted out

we are tossed away on howls of orange wind into a
welcome green trance.

"Mainlining" whilst meditating on a crucifix

Solitary
the moon is weeping crystal,
Welcoming
grey clouds which are a caress

For her eyes
glazed like glass spheres,
The dialogue is with silk veils
like the nothingness which beckons death

into twilight, we are tossed into whirls of dust.

He rolls-up a shirtsleeve
the needle marks are like stigmata,
Brown and purple bruises that glare
as shadows weep across the terrain of whispers.

Glancing heavenwards
our light is dancing into the voids of night,
Silhouettes are roaming around this room, the Word
is suspended on a cross of wood, emaciated bodies are

sacrificed to this fire which is never to be quenched by
the dew?

The chess board consists of 64 squares, are you one?

The chipped chess pieces, the pawns, chant their
abhorrence at the
Smooth and uninterrupted movement of both a Rook
and the Queen,
At the fatal power of the Kings demise which terminates
their game,
He was checkmated because of impotence and
ineptitude, you didn't
Avoid being mated: the Grand Master who is
reincarnated as a flea
Studies the game, metamorphosis's himself into sticky
brown slime,
He then oozes onto the board, only godless like the
inexorable tides,
The tacky mucus seeps its way into the pristine
chequered surface.

Did you lead a chequered life or as cramped as the
pawns, chipped
And clipped, never raced from A8 to R8, only P-K4*, an
anticipated
Opening and so is everything else, just predictable like
the ticking of
A chess clock, you 'play by the rules', 'stay on the
board'; secure, its
Death-in-life because the brown snot is caustic, it will
erode you until
Deranged the only option is to plead for checkmate, you
64 squares.
*The juxtaposition of the two systems of chess notation:
a) Algebraic and b) English is intentional.

Lines on William Burroughs' concept of 'death-in-life'

Square
hearts had
stopped, they were

Just
rusty bilge
pumps, someone turned

The
switch off,
what a turn-on

Never
dug that
scene with America

And
atom bombs,
chant with those

Of
us who
have a different

                    sound
                         and
                              song
to the hooded-snake death dirge, breathe an autumn
                             wind
                    of
                pure
                    purgation,
                howl
                    cathartic

Icarus Still Flies

            baby   burnout
            buzz   madness.

            He had placed
            enigma in caps.
                              opened
that cap, cooked it,
                                        fixed it,
again, again, hazy.
DECONDITIONED HIMSELF FROM
STATE SUBLIMNIAL MIND MANIPULATION,
He had the sweet-death golden flight of Icarus, also the
endless labour of Sisyphus.

            Illusion, allusion and delusion.

Crimson crystals are burning
                    pulsating
                         embers
                              gobbling

Inferno,
is this a solitary illusion like blood?
                         stained
                              sacred

Sacrament
or a academic allusion to a sanitised
                    Dante,
                         mistaken

because
Although this may not scold your flesh
                         forget us

Damned

At your peril purgatory will not cleanse

you, Hell

is

where

we weep wild like galloping horses, just snorting this chaos,
the delusion is that heaven existed, no haven or home
for us.

Speaking of viral poetry...

'Language is a virus from outer space. ... The author is simply a node on a network, through which ideas pass.'

~ William Burroughs: 'The Ticket that Explodes' (1962).

That fatigue can no longer frighten us like the frozen ice sheets in the mind,
 it is beyond any vestige or manifestation of fear as glaring of sun drills eyes.

The black petals begin to fold inwards
when a gaze is or isn't fixed, tangles of twisted thorns of a tight thistle bush are forests of emptiness, viral poetry is written and formed into lakes of ice, from ice is refined the pure crystals that are polished into those old cold stars,
they had imploded long ago creating the gulping black holes, babies' mouths
who drink from a black nipple which oozes dark milk, its ancient not nectar,
It is the ingestion of the 'Other', us as dark subject, objectification is unmade.

Promenaded people you wake-up and don't think black holes are empty, scabby fingers are grasping the bourgeois hand and it shivers with revulsion, grey suited exorcists wail 'demon get out', but we existed for eons before Eden or logos; our word is an infectious virus. For you are totally helpless, we have convinced your best philosophers since Epicurus and inspired the poet Sappho, then lit the fuse around October 1917. We are the Virus made word, made material in your universe, we are cellular.

Nigel Pearce

**Some variations on a theme of unrequited love
inspired by reading William Carlos Williams**

a).
In autumn
wind blew golden
leaves like her sorrow.

b).
Have drowned
in her lunar silhouette
to wander in our shadow.

Icarus Still Flies

Lines on Brigitte M:

(a leading member of the Socialist Patients Collective[1])

A chill and steel grimace glares and stares
from the tarnished goblet from which she

                                        didn't drink.

Substitutionism is easy in class struggle,
she didn't substitute emotions with zeros

                                        never drunk,

Replace the proletariat with a vanguard?
but never replace authenticity with shit

                                        of oppression.

Kill a revolutionist with a gun or tablets
but they will rise like your fear of death.

                                        Many drunk

From this cup with Brigitte M, not china
tea-services of the oppressor; she smiled

                                        then gulped

That red wine of love, it intoxicated her
with a fantastic desire to destroy Daddy
            in all his manifestations.

She was an incarnation, a realization and
beatification of insurrection, her gun fired
            lemon butterflies
                    of
love.

---

[1]S.P.K. (Socialist Patients Collective) was an armed group of
Marxists who had been diagnosed with mental health
problems. They formed the 'second generation' of the R.A.F.
(Red Army Faction) in West Germany. Many, including
Brigitte M, spent decades in secure hospitals and prisons.
Refusing to renounce their beliefs the SPK members were
hen mental health legislation or denied parole for long
periods..

Reaction Poem No 1

Radical rightist rant assailed 'I' spider poet on gloomy
day at an Arts centre: hatred was spewed, almost
ejaculated out of a square ex - head's mouth, said: 'I'm
clean and sober and a Christian', his liturgy then
erupted as fascist litany:

> 'I'm fucking proud to be British,
> I'm bloody British
> And if you fucking red

bastards

> Don't like it here then piss off.'

A molten roar of a rush remembered must have surged
in his veins. I instead smelt that stench of the benighted
vermin whose ovens burnt and belched the incinerated
bodies of comrades and Jews, gays and the mental
patients[2]. 'I' spider poet running in 70's riots[3] inhaled the
intoxicating scent of the flower called revolutionary
praxis, that is class warfare. Remember struggles, in
those now closed psychiatric hospitals, that would
quickly end with sharp a jab of Largactal[4] in clenched

---

[2]German fascists incinerated millions including 6 million
Jewish people, Marxist   'comrades' ('reds'), homosexual
and lesbian people and also mentally ill patients who were
gassed in mobile chambers. This happened in sealed lorries
which travelled between some mental hospitals into which
cyanide fumes were pumped; beginning around 1935 it
occurred before the 'Final Solution' (this was the attempted
elimination of European Jewry).

[3]* There were many violent demonstrations between fascists
and Marxists during the 1970's in UK.

[4]* Largactal was a strong sedative given to psychiatric
patients, sometimes by intramuscular injection, at one time.

legs, like midnight. The fascists can masquerade as Christians, but behind their mask lurks the sinister shadow figure: Social Kulak[5]

NOTE: In 1960/70's there was an active 'Christian-Marxist Dialogue' e.g. Camilo   Torres was a priest, a theologian and also an active pro-Marxist revolutionary. Although for the last 30 years some Christian fundamentalists have used their interpretation of 'biblical text' for 'rightist' political purposes. Today for some preachers it has become a convenient mask for hatred. As in the 1980's many used it as a tool against Marxists and in favour of 'free- market' capitalism. Of course, ultimately, like all established belief systems it is a 'reflex' of the dominant ideology. However it is possible to argue that within a clearly defined historical period and for a well delineated social group within an oppressed class religion can become a 'resistance ideology'; see E. P. Thompson: 'The Making of the English Working Class' for an analysis of the anti-capitalist role of some Protestant sects during the 19th century.

---

[5]Social Kulak is a hybrid term which has two roots: 1) Kulaks were pro-
  Tsarist/ruling class landed peasants who opposed and then declined after the
  Marxist October 1917 Revolution 2) 'Social Fascist' was a specific term used by
  some Marxists to describe 'class collaborators' in Germany in the period
  leading up to the establishment of fascism in 1933. Hence the term 'Social Kulak'

Nigel Pearce

Summer of love

(a villanelle).

Time melts; we thawed a frosty reality to dissolve ice
with our love,
Our eyes whose dilated pupils could swallow any
hardened gaze,
(You fell across this hallucinogenic Cosmos, these stars
tumble).

We crucified the betrayal of damned love and stared to
humble
That dark spark, we conceived this just like evaporating
into haze,
Time melts; we thawed a frosty reality to dissolve ice
with our love,

I touched with delicate fingers the clasp on your eyes to
unbuckle
A stream, the purple fragrance of humming, a goddess
was ablaze,
(You fell across this hallucinogenic Cosmos, these stars
tumble).

You crumpled into a sphere of sighs encircled by white
light, a dove
Whose wings were caressed as we dived into the sun in
a daze,
Time melts; we thawed a frosty reality to dissolve ice
with our love.

Our song was vibrating into weeping trees, nectar
dripping, suckle
Each other's ancient milk which is a sacred libation with
soft praise,

Icarus Still Flies

(You fell across this hallucinogenic Cosmos, these stars
tumble).

Tangerine gasp intertwine in a frenzy of breath, it falls
from above,
Then we lie exhausted in a grave, our bodies consumed,
but raised.
Time melts; we thawed a frosty reality to dissolve ice
with our love,
(You fell across this hallucinogenic Cosmos, these stars
tumble).

Nigel Pearce

The creation myth of Purusha in the Satapatha Brahamana (c.800BC)[6]

*Our minds may try and cancel, attempt to blank, this
switch was flicked 800 B.C., he had over 1,000 eyes
And heads, Purusha was total visual, complete sight,
absolute cognition: dived into night without oblivion.*

*But a core of zero he only became a number through
introspection, digging that nothingness until he floats
Around a crown of Lotus flowers, here he discovered
the warmth and softness which is Yoni, he luxuriated
 'I am.'*

*But like poets at dawn without a pen and paper he had
only desire, he tore himself with pure golden energy to
Create 'Other', lover, she became a daughter, they were
black and white flaming water and running fire: joined.*

*This act created you and you and me, so says this myth.
ashamed she ran like a gazelle fleeing a lion, he would
Become a gazelle, again and again he deceived her
until
they had produced each and every animal on this Earth.*

~ N.S.Pearce.

Notes.

---

[6]This is only one version of several Purusha creation myths
which occurred over a period of time, they are diverse in
content?

1) The earliest representation of the Lotus in art is in a crown of
        flowers that adorned a figure of the Earth Goddess which was
        discovered in the Indus Valley. It dates from 3,000 B.C.
2) In Hindu mythology the Lotus flower represents the feminine
        life-force and is the symbol of the Yoni or female generative
        organs.
3) Simone de Beauvoir, a French feminist, said: 'In women is
        incarnated in positive form the lack that the existent (male)
carries in his heart.' ~ Simone de Beauvoir: 'The Second Sex' (1949).

Nigel Pearce

Psalm to the poetry of joy

The moon rises like mist distilled from a burnt river
To whirl with her humming until the bonds unravel,
Now she is caressing her smile into radiant morning,
Her dust is lingering it sprinkles onto dormant souls
Of night awaking our song of love to a golden dawn,
The poet's pen is dipping into this chalice of nectar,
We wander across pages with infinity and innocence
A dance with the light and shadows of sacred ritual,
Psalm of joy to a pristine moon and the drowsy sun.

Your eyes are shining

(a prose-poem)

Those eyes shine with emerald green in our trip again, it has the certainty
with which a frost in winter will freeze a blade of grass and is sure as a
decaying autumn leaf of gold is trampled under the boots of eternity. But,
my goddess of the lunar wailing, your perfume intoxicates the psyche of
this poet as he is falling into a labyrinth of dreams. Here shadows are like
obscured glass splinters which pierce the mind, we are cast into a fallibility
of chained genes, they hang like globules of honey draped on a derelict
hive. It is here we return step by step, through the honeycombs, past the
corpses of dead worker bees to the queen who nestles her sterile eggs and
beyond to the primordial swamp, there our stunted fingers clutch each other
in a grasp of love. Your eyes are still as we come down again, so softly into
our folds of tissue.

She is the bridge across the river of Death

A vulture sweeps on hidden currents seeking carrion.
We cuddled death and squeezed it out of a rock; the
vibes began gliding around a hill of lush green grass
overshadowed by
                         A Gold Phallus,
The phallus ejaculated the words of the dull with a force
that shot them high into the
sky where glazed eyes are blind, drilled them into the
side of the head where dilated
pupils are gobbling madness into their depths and then
a pink fish gulped their dirge.

Flying beyond the cruel clasp of fire and reaching the icy
shady spheres where there
was a river of sparkling glass which was fluid and flowed
fast, a woman clothed with black robes approached, her
face was deathly pale and her eyes dark and sad, she
said: 'take my hand', we floated on and skimmed across
the surface of the river that sparks,
her whisper is melody: 'this is your end, dissolve atom
by atom in my tunnel of night'.

A meditation on Andy Warhol's 'Factory'[7]

Many had entered this company of the joyful and mad
because they wrote and did speed[8] enticed they were
sucked into a dark-room, dragged in but
Spewed out when in pain; some fixed and wrote, others
painted after a hit,
There were those who wailed their ink or paint onto
paper like orgasms of
A moon's second rising: some were green-eyed with
their claws extended
Scratching each other in the desert and simultaneously
drunk from an oasis.

Their profane families of distrust were crucified and
sacrificed, coffined
permitting poets to descend from their cross without that
burnt stigmata.

Some wandered and wised their way out, went to
labyrinths of communes
as hashish somnambulists, but alert they kept a pen and
paper within reach.

The barbiturate[9] bard taught to fumble, stumble and
mumble proclaims:

---

[7]'The Factory' was Andy Warhol's 'underground' Arts project
and a counter-culture 'hang out' in 1960's New York.

[8]Speed' was a term commonly employed to describe
amphetamine based stimulants such as Benzedrine which
were widely used in the 'counter-culture' to increase the
intensity and duration of wakefulness. Interestingly Jean-Paul
Sartre, the French philosopher and novelist said: 'it lights up
the sun in my mind.' However use can also lead to a
permanent psychosis (insanity).

'I can recall and write about the verse they wrote in his Methedrine[10] Ark'.

---

[9]'Barbiturate' was a class of drugs used by psychiatrists during the 1960's to sedate mental patients, but they were also used in the 'counter-culture' where they would be mixed with alcohol or injected directly into the vein when money was tight, both methods lead to many accidental deaths. It was also taken orally to reduce the 'come down' from stimulants such as Methadrine.

[10]'Methadrine' is a potent form of amphetamine which was the drug of choice at 'The Factory'. Here the phrase: 'to take a poke' was coined for an intramuscular injection of Methadrine. Hence the incidence of speed induced psychosis there was quite significant.

An incarnation of Sappho[11] and her friend accidentally OD

Some spit with spite and call it love, but not us,
Not in a temple of Aphrodite, here Sappho tends
A flame which brushes her lips, they are burning
And red...now purple as the heroin hits hard like
A hammer thumping its heat up the arm into that
Galaxy of welcoming brain cells, the hypodermic
Hangs limp from her arm, I gently draw the spike
Out of the bruised vein, her arm flops diagonally
Across an orange cotton shirt, I clean the syringe
By rhythmically flushing water in and out and
Finally squirt the crimson juice into blue china
Bowl; next prepare my hit, we uncurl in a temple
Of Aphrodite which is where lovers can purr softly,
The floor opens like a gaping mouth and swallows.

---

[11]Sappho was a Greek poet who lived around 600 B.C. She performed the duties of a priestess of Aphrodite on the island of Lesbos. The philosopher Plato described her as 'the tenth muse'. Her poetry expressed love for a circle of women friends. One Pope, in the Middle Ages, considered her work so subversive that he ordered it should be burnt.

Can you explain fascism by psychoanalysis NO! Organize the workers' militias!

Those fascists are drunks lying in the gutter with their icy blue eyes blind to the stars, like the animated dead in a vacuous chill morning covered in last night's vomit, it congeals, reeks as Nazi's lie in their bath until the water becomes chill, awash with decay and scum, afraid to the pull plug in case a frantic rat leaps out.

Poor people should ponder we are strong composing our own songs of solidarity, it's the petty-bourgeoisie[12] warps those symphonies of primal pristine perfection.

Electra is pitiable as she stumbles through the zone looking for another hit of warmth and death deforming and distorted for in the unconscious Pater did not genuflect before her thorn garlanded shrine, she has worn the crown of thorns and used it to maim herself, is she hypnotised Caucasian Kali incarnate: No!

Can you explain a fascist by their nightmares? No we choose either Left or Right,

---

[12]This is a reference to the class 'petty-bourgeois' as an objective class relationship rather than to individual members of a particular socio-economic class. It is sandwiched between the two main contending classes of the epoch of 'late-capitalism'; which are the bourgeoisie and the proletariat and, therefore, is not totally committed to capitalism like the bourgeois or dialectically opposed to it and in favour of a classless society as is the proletariat. The 'petty-bourgeoisie' holds instead an intermediate position and therefore contains the seed of a social system that is neither capitalist nor socialist i.e. fascist and barbarian. To achieve these ends the fascists must smash organized 'labour' and enlist elements of 'finance capital' (banking money) to impose their tyranny over the majority

the masses awake from sleep, no dream analysis now
it's who controls streets?
workers bound by a shadow may become fascists, don't
reduce this to therapy,
one is a mental malady, but the only red remedy for
fascism is a workers' militia[13].

---

[13]A quotation from Leon Trotsky illustrates this point: 'The struggle against fascism is basically a political struggle which needs a militia just as a strike needs pickets. Basically, the picket is the embryo of the workers' militia.'

A man became an egg;

(surrealist poem).

There was a spectral man who hid in a physical frame,
he roamed like a grounded vulture across anonymous
plains of concrete, there is no harvest of golden corn or
pleasant deer too inspire the poet here, only the arched
acridness of the hard, the junkies huddled in alleyways
wailing with junk sickness: once a thin and translucent
membrane formed herself around the man and he just
touched it tingling rebirth, she shyly encrusted herself
but
      egg
          shells
                are
                      thin,
                            egg
                                boxes
never are quite right like papier-mâché disintegrating
in the rain, the shell shattered and she madly distorted
herself and became his yoke: both essence and burden.

An artist with eyes like black oceans painted the egg in
beautiful gold, blue and bright crimson: he ate the egg,
yoke flowed out dark as bitter blood into the pen of the
poet who writes as a serpent who has just been
uncoiled.

The ice-box

This is a box within a box, a world within a world, a house which is typical of many found within suburbia. It is brown bricked, anonymous and almost transmits hymns of praise to some tarnished copper god of mediocrity. In the kitchen of this house stands a fridge, it looks white and prosaic. Open the fridge door and at the top on the right is a sky blue ice-box, it has three white stars to confirm the adequacy of its freezing capacity. Inside the ice-box is a rectangular tray which is divided into squares, each can be filled with water and then frozen to produce the perfect ice-cube. This can then be dropped into a frosted pink glass which wraps around it, add fruit juice and there is the perfect chilled drink.

A son frequently opens the fridge door and pulls down the sky blue ice-box flap and peeps inside. He examines the frosted walls which, paradoxically, burn his fingers; they are almost burnt with the coldness. It is in this world of ice-cubes that he discovers another dimension which exists separately from, but is intrinsically attached, to the ebb and flow of everyday life. The son's mother had died some years ago and he had been left the house, he did not sell it because there wasn't really anywhere else to go. The son had an unusual relationship with the ice-cubes in the fridge finding great comfort in popping two out from the tray and holding them in his hands until they were numb and the ice-cubes dissolved into water.

The living-room of this box within a box was bare, no carpet, no furnishings or pictures. However glaring at him was a gas fire. It had short brown steel legs with one at each end to support it. A copper pipe stuck up through the floor boards and was connected to the fire. The fire itself was coloured in two tones of brown, light-brown at the bottom and around the sides of the gas jets and above was dark brown. The shelf which was on top of the whole apparatus and rested against the wall had white plastic knops at each end, one is to turn-on and ignite the gas and the other is to control the flow of gas in order to regulate the temperature. This fire concerned the son greatly, it almost dominated him. He didn't like the hissing of the gas or the flickering flames and the brief smell of gas at ignition caused him much anxiety. He felt little or no choice but to constantly check and check again that the gas was burning correctly and there was no leak. With the certainty of the tides his life became enslaved to this gas-fire. The only respite was allowing the ice-cubes to melt in his hands.

Just as the season's motion is inevitable the gas fire developed a leak. Fortunately the son was elsewhere when the explosion tore through the house destroying it and its anonymity. It no longer looked like all the other houses in the cul-de-sac. The fridge was badly damaged and thought to no longer fulfil any useful task; it was taken to the local tip. The ice-cubes turned into water, but a more profound metamorphosis took place: a voice said:

'My son, there is no longer any need to worry.'

The water had leaked from the ice-box and out of the fridge into the rubbish of the tip in which it germinated a seed planted at the beginning of Time. The shoot will push its way up through the waste and bloom next spring, a snow-drop.

Psychiatric nurse, try reading some Dostoevsky

The psychiatric nurse wears a smile of roses,
But when he opens his mouth only the thorns
Show, they rip into us as mercury is rising up the
Thermometer, but we are like Mercury, we are
The messengers of words, of communication
Between mortality and the void, our emotional
Temperature is wrong, our perceptions are askew,
So chant the nurses as they prostrate themselves
Before an idol 'THE SELF' in its glory and feel one
Of the few, a mental health professional, we break the
Shackles on the nurse's ego and drag them from their
Shallows of grey bourgeois murk, then of course they
React and start behaving like enflamed flamingos, with
Moments of insight here, incisive understanding there,
And then in wonder a diagnosis: nurse read Dostoevsky
And step into his weird world of underground people.

Book Review

'On Dostoevsky.' – Susan Leigh Anderson

Anderson's philosophical analysis of the ideas which motivated, or at least developed in, Dostoevsky novels is stimulating if not entirely convincing. Correctly she places Dostoevsky in the milieu of Kierkegaard and Nietzsche. However she then degenerates into an almost ritualistic denouncement of Dostoevsky's early revolutionary socialism for which he was taken to the point of execution and spent four years in a penal colony being deprived of books or writing materials. However the main thread of her thesis is based on ethics which she claims was also Dostoevsky's major interest and is indeed of importance. Dostoevsky's philosophical question was: How you can reconcile free will in the 'libertarian sense' with the concept of a God who is omniscient? The consequence is that God must have decided that evil in the world is a price worth paying for freedom. Anderson suggests that, for Dostoevsky, the solution was to create 'absolute values'. I, like Anderson, reject 'Ethical Relativism' but do not believe that the ethical values necessary to lead an 'good' life are enshrined in the heavens, indeed that seems a form of human alienation. The values necessary to lead an ethical life are rooted within Humanity itself, but these are distorted by oppression and exploitation and can only flourish in a socialist society. Dostoevsky describes his ideal world as: 'universal communion of wo/men...the maintenance of complete liberty.'
These things can only be created by the proletariat sweeping away oppression and exploitation.

Existentialism and the role of the poet today

> "*Vertigo is anguish to the extent that I am afraid not of falling over the precipice, but of throwing myself over.*"
> ~ Jean-Paul Sartre.

Existentialism, unlike other philosophical systems, stresses the subjective experience of human beings in our daily lives. An early reference to this problem of everyday life is in Blasé Pascal's: Pensees. He argued that without a God our lives would be absurd and sad, people would create goals and "work", but all these endeavours would be meaningless. To escape this situation Pascal rejected atheism.

Kierkegaard and Nietzsche can be seen as the founders of the Existentialist movement, although they didn't use the term to describe themselves. Both lived in the 19th century and, following Pascal's work, were interested in the problems of meaninglessness. However, they went beyond Pascal's and asserted a new freedom for human beings:

> "*truth is subjectivity.*'
> ~ Kierkegaard.

This means that the most important thing for a human being is the inner relationship we have with existence: an inner relationship with "absurdity."

Nietzsche proclaimed: "*the death of God.*"

His words would shake and transform the experience of Western civilisation from the late 19th century onwards. When D.H.Lawrence read Nietzsche he said:

*"If there is nothing to believe in, we must,
therefore undermine everything."*
~D.H.Lawrence.

We can see the themes of both Kierkegaard and
Nietzsche running through 20th century Existentialism.

However, I would like briefly to examine the literary
existentialists and the rise of a concomitant dissident
sub-culture. The experience of "absurdity" and feelings
of guilt without a source are explored in the literature of
Franz Kafka. His characters are accused of crimes they
have no knowledge of by anonymous authorities, a kind
of nightmare of patriarchal societies without a concept of
forgiveness.

Dostoevsky's novel 'Crime and Punishment' is about
those who commit apparently irrational acts and live on
the margins of society, those who are cast out of the
social system: the outsiders.

In the 1950's and 1960's existentialist writing again
became the literature of authenticity and was articulating
a sub-culture which rejected the artistic forms and
values of commodity capitalism. The poetry of Allen
Ginsberg and the surrealistic novels of William
Burroughs became known as 'Beat' writing. It embraced
the spontaneity of the black jazz musicians that they
admired.

Their emphasis on "authenticity" was inspired by
existentialism and they became a significant cultural
force. 'Beat' culture was bohemian in nature and
advocated disengaging with "straight" or mainstream
society and living in a dissident sub-culture.

In the 1960's and 1970's a "counter-culture" of people
inspired by the writing and life-style of the 'Beats', by

Timothy Leary advocating the use of L.S.D. as a means of attaining a chemical "Enlightenment", the rise of revolutionary social movements and Jean-Paul Sartre's existentialist philosophy becoming widely read all combined to create a crisis in international capitalism and its agents of social control such as patriarchal authority and the nuclear family.

The shackles on our consciousness were being cast off and the "wage-slavery" (Marx) of late-capitalism was being challenged by those who were disaffected and by the revolutionary sections of the proletariat.

I would now like to explore Jean-Paul Sartre's existentialism in a little more detail. A core concept is that:

"*Existence precedes essence.*"
~ Jean- Paul Sartre

As there is not a primal source to create a human essence, because "God is dead.", then human beings are confronted by the question:"what is the nature of my existence?" For Sartre we create our own "essence" or "being":

"*Human reality can receive its ends neither from outside or from so calledinner nature.*"
~Jean- Paul Sartre.

We, therefore, create our own identities which are the source of existential freedom, but this causes anxiety in an absurd world:

   "*it is anguish that wo/man gets from the consciousness of freedom*"
~Jean-Paul Sartre.

But this "freedom" and the "anguish" it provokes can be overwhelming and we can retreat into what Sartre called "Bad Faith".

"we flee anguish by attempting to apprehend ourselves from without as an "Other" or as a thing." ~ Jean-Paul Sartre.

This "Other" can be the people we meet or, as Simone de Beauvoir argued in her study 'The Second Sex', that in patriarchal social systems women are perceived as the "Other" of the male subject.

What is the role of the poet and artist today? We should write about the "absurd" and relate to those who live on the periphery of society. The writer, to quote Sartre must always engage "on the side of freedom". He developed this idea in 'What is Literature' by arguing that committed literature must always create imagined worlds against the exploitation of 'late-capitalism' and, therefore, confront all forms of oppression e.g. homophobia and racism. The freedom that the writer has is itself constrained by the boundaries of any given epoch because art, like any other ideological manifestation, is the product of complex socio-economic and political relationships. Sartre was to argue that existentialism itself was only "an ideological moment" within Marxism and that

"Marxism is the one philosophy of our time which we cannot go beyond."
~ Jean-Paul Sartre

The exploitation of the international proletariat and its resistance to oppression today resembles that which Sartre and his generation experienced in the 1950's when French imperialism was being opposed in Algeria; they made a stand against the imperialists then. Again poets, artists and their supporters are in the vanguard of the global struggle against bourgeois hegemony and its agents. Our task is clear...

"...we must re-conquer humanity with Marxism."~ Jean-Paul Sartre.

Nigel Pearce

On Marxist economic theory and the global crisis today

> *'Modern bourgeois society, with its relations of production,of exchange and of property, a society that has conjured upsuch gigantic means of production and of exchange, is like the sorcerer who is no longer able to control the powers ofthe nether world that he has called up by his spells.'*
>
> ~ Karl Marx

The world is today being rocked by the largest economic crisis since 'The Wall Street Crash' of 1929 and may collapse into a recession as deep as 'The Great Depression' of the 1930's which followed that banking crisis. Then the balance of global forces was weighted against revolutionary socialists and their capacity to lead the working class to victory with the creation of a 'Workers State' and an eventual transition to communism. i.e. a classless society without the existence of private property. The consequence of this failure of revolutionary socialism was the triumph of fascism in Germany and the consolidation of counter-revolutionary Stalinism in Russia. Today we again look over the edge of an abyss, our choice:

> *'Socialism or barbarism'.* ~ Rosa Luxemburg.

As we gaze at the bewildered bourgeois politicians and their confused academic advisors one thing is absolutely clear: quite simply capitalism does not work, it is bankrupt as an economic system. There is much talk of fiscal stimulation for the economy, but these ideas are concepts within bourgeois economics devised by Keynes during the 1930's in his 'General Theory of

Employment, Interest and Money" as a solution to the 'Great Depression' and are now being applied to crumpling capitalism today. His ideas were embraced by the ruling class as a solution to their plight in the 1930's and then many non-Marxist 'Social Democratic' theorists and parties also agreed with his ideas. The essence of his theory was that the working class is not to be blamed for the scourge of mass unemployment and that it is the duty of the state to stimulate growth in the economy to create jobs and growth and therefore save capitalism from complete debacle. In Keynes' view, during a 'Depression', when consumers are limited in their capacity to spend and therefore expand the economy by buying commodities it was necessary to create public investments to achieve state fueled economic growth. However the underlying ideological aspect of Keynesianism is that the ruling class is concerned of the effect that mass unemployment could have on the prospects for capitalism surviving; the mass unemployed could be organized by socialist revolutionaries and the system which functions in the interests of the class who Keynes represented overthrown.

Indeed the preparations for World. War II and the central role of the state in driving the war economy convinced many throughout the world on both the Left as well as the Right that Keynesian economic theory was the solution to the problems of capitalism. The 'Post-War Boom' even convinced some Marxists that 'capitalism had produced the goods' (Marcuse) and the epoch of crisis at the heart of capitalism was over. But during the 1970's+1980's it became clear the Keynesianism had just been a palliative as a new recession loomed and the class struggle again intensified. The solution the bourgeois economists of that era hoped to treat the problem of economic crisis and inflation with was Monetarism because Keynes' ideas had failed. The most committed disciple of this ideology was Margaret Thatcher. Monetarism was to a large extent derived from the Chicago School of Economics and in particular from the work of Milton Friedman. He argued that:

> 'The Great Depression, like most other periods of severe unemployment, was produced by government mismanagement rather than by any instability of the private economy.'
>
> ~ Milton Friedman

This is a profoundly anti-Marxist orientation because for Marx there is an 'Inherent tendency of the rate of profit to fall' (Marx) in capitalist economies. Hence for Friedman the problem was 'big government' and the regulation of free markets'. He believed that supply and demand would come into harmony by 'price equilibrium' i.e. price of goods balance the market. Friedman believed that a Keynesian solution of state intervention in the economy led to an inflationary increase in the money supply. These ideas, once accepted, by large sections of the ruling class lead to vicious attacks on workers living standards and attacks on the Welfare Statethroughout the 1980's,90's and indeed the 'New Labour' project was just a Friedmanite wolf in sheep's clothing.

However today capitalism or what we can call the 'neo-liberalist mode of capitalism' faces another 'Depression' and once again the Keynesian medicine is being administered: but the truth is both Keynesism and Monetarism have failed in the past. This is because they treat the dysfunctional symptoms of capitalism rather than the problem itself which is capitalism and its inherent contradictions.

Is there an alternative to these two discredited economic theories? In the 'Preface to 'Capital' Marx writes:

> *'It is the ultimate aim of this work to lay bare
> the economic law of motion of modern society,
> i.e. a capitalist, bourgeois society'.'*
> ~ Karl Marx.

Marx's analysis begins with an observation that in the capitalist mode of production the 'commodity' is predominant. How is a 'commodity' created, how does it gain its 'value'? Marx explains this with the 'labour theory of value' in which he maintains that 'labour power' or the worker creates 'value' rather than the power of machines. Marx elaborates on this and argues that it is the 'socially necessary labour time' (which is the amount of labour required to create a particular 'good' with the average amount of labour using the average level of techniques and working with average effort) that creates 'value' rather than the laws of supply and demand:

> *'As values, all commodities are only definite
> masses of congealed labour time'.*
> ~ Karl Marx

So workers create the value of a commodity, but this is divided into 'use-value' which is the usefulness gained from this product and the 'exchange value' which is the pricemeasured in labour time of this commodity. As Lenin explained:

> *'A commodity is, in the first place, a thing that
> satisfies a human want; in the second place, it is a
> thing that can be exchanged for another thing. The
> utility of a thing is its use-value…Exchange-value
> presents itself…as a relation…to a certain number*

*of use-values of one sort which are exchanged for
a number of use-values of another sort'.*

- V.I.Lenin

What then is 'Capital'? There are three general laws
discovered by Marx:

1) The general formula for commodity production was
C-M-C

(commodity-money-commodity) here money allows
the circulation of commodities as one commodity is sold
for another.

2) However the general formula of 'money' is M-C-M

(money-commodity- money) this is when a
commodity is bought with money and then sold.

3) Money only becomes 'Capital' when a good has
greater value that is realized in selling it for a profit. M-
C-M+1

(money-commodity-money+1).

So what is the essence of this 'profit' or 'surplus value'?
It is the 'labour power' needed to create the commodity
for which the worker gets a wage which is less than the
total amount of 'value' he has created, therefore
allowing the capitalist to siphon off the rest as 'surplus
value' and realize it as profit.

Today capitalism is staggering like a drunken person
looking for his home, but completely bemused, doesn't
know what direction to take. The Banking Crisis was a
symptom of this befuddled person but not the cause.
Marx understood the source and explained it in 'Law of

the tendency of the rate of profit to fall', as Marx points out:

> *'The rate of self-expansion of capitalism or the rate of profit, its fall...appears as a threat to the whole capitalist process'.*

> ~ Karl Marx

Essentially this 'law of profit to fall' is quite simple to understand. Marx takes the two elements in production; the first he calls 'constant capital' it includes machines, buildings etc, he refers to this, also, as 'dead labour' because it doesn't produce value. The second element in production he calls 'variable capital', this is the labour power which creates value and he sometimes refers to this as 'living labour'. Because the capitalist has constantly to invest in more productive 'constant capital' in relation to 'variable labour,' because he must compete with other capitalists, this in the short term increases the amount of value a worker creates, but in the long term this investment in 'dead labour' which does not produce value acts as a weight dragging down the amount of 'living labour' which produces less overall value and therefore has an adverse impact on profits.

The logic of capitalism has created the economic 'Depression' and the working class must prepare the inevitable struggles which face us, these will sometimes be 'defensive' but on other occasions the proletariat will go on the offensive. What we are facing now is not just a crisis of 'neo-liberalism' but of the mode of production of capitalism itself.

'We make our own history, but in the first place under very definite presuppositions and conditions. Among these economic ones are fairly decisive. But the

*political ones and even the traditions which haunt
human minds, also play a part, but not the decisive one.'*

- Fredrick Engels

'The working class is revolutionary or it is nothing'

- Karl Marx

Heinrich Heine: poet and revolutionary.

'Ask me not what I have, but what I am.'

– Heinrich Heine

Heinrich Heine was born 1797 in Germany. He was both an important poet in the German 'Romantic' tradition and a revolutionary socialist. These two combine to make Heine pertinent today and a significant figure in proletarian literature. Why? The answer is to be located in the complex interactions between socio-economic forces in the context of History', we may define this as 'Historical Materialism', and the role of the poet in 'alienating' bourgeois conditions i.e. in the relations of Capitalism. Firstly this analysis will briefly define the methodology described as Historical Materialism which is then applied to the crucial question of the 'alienated 'Romantic poet'. Four main areas of inquiry will be examined in that context: a) biographical details and Heine's textual material b) the place of Heine in the context of the friendship with Marx and Engels, c) the significance of his role as a poet in the revolutionary movement, d) and finally draw the lessons for the oppressed today we can draw from Heine.

Therefore I will illustrate the methodological orientation for this study which is 'Historical Materialism'. Basically there are two essential philosophical categories which have, indeed, sub-sections. They are 'Idealism' and Materialism':

> '*The great basic question of all philosophy is that concerning the relation of thinking and being...which the philosophers have split into two*

Nigel Pearce

> great camps...the camp of Idealism and the
> various schools of Materialism.
>
> - Engels: *'Ludwig Feuerbach.'*

I would like to stress here that the terms 'Idealism' and 'Materialism' are here employed in a specific usage is which described by Maurice Cornforth:

'1) Idealism asserts that the material world is dependent on the spiritual.

2) Idealism asserts that that spirit, or mind, or idea, can and do exist in separation from matter.

3) Idealism asserts that there exists a realm of the mysterious and unknowable, 'above', or 'beyond' or 'behind' what can be ascertained and known by perception, experience and science.'

> - Maurice Cornforth: *'Materialism and the Dialectical Method''*.

This is not just an abstract debate but is one that has a direct consequence on the future of humanity because mistakes in theory lead to errors on practice and if the 'Universal Class', the proletariat and their vanguard party make them the repercussions are immense. If we choose an incorrect methodology, a wrong way of looking and understanding the world we cannot make the correct 'concrete analysis of concrete situations' (Lenin). So what is 'Materialism': firstly it is the instrument which the working class and its Party arm themselves in the class struggle. Philosophy is partisan; you are either a reactionary or a revolutionary, you are either for the crumbling social order or against it as Marx noted: 'All History is the history of class struggle' and as

Trotsky reflected: 'Capitalism has entered its death agony'. Secondly as is apparent in the contrast to 'Idealism' the Materialist schools see 'change' for as Engels noted 'reality is matter in motion. More that that the materialists believe the world is knowable to the masses not just the privileged elite of priests and mystics. So when you apply materialism to History the school of thought to embrace is Historical Materialism, the theory of the oppressed, indeed the hope for humanity, but which is founded in material reality. Lenin, of course, encapsulates the whole conception with insight and theoretical penetration:

'The history of philosophy has shown clearly that Marxism contains nothing of the least resemblance to 'sectarianism' in the sense of any closed up, fossilized doctrine...On the contrary: The whole genus of Marx consists in his giving answers to questions which the progressive thinking of humanity had already posed.'

- Lenin: *'The Three Sources and Component* Parts *of Marxism'*

Having established the method used in this paper it is necessary to examine the role of the poet, the estranged poet. Trotsky had commented that poets have to:

'...reshape the world of feelings. Not everybody is capable of that.'

- Trotsky: *'Literature and Revolution'*

Heine also commented on the estranged poet in bourgeois society:

'Since the heart of the poet is the central point of the world it must at present times be woefully torn. Those who are able to boost that their hearts have remained whole are only admitting that they have a prosaic narrow heart'.

- Heine

Heine was a poet in the tradition of German romanticism which was initially a feudal reaction to the French revolution and the English industrial revolution and it flourished during the reaction of its collapse. But some had supported the French Revolution and were profoundly disappointed by its failure. Hence among this group of poets and intellectuals appeared a revolutionary dimension to German Romanticism that began to rise of which Heine was a part. Therefore, but avoiding idealist analysis, we can understand how poets such as Heine embraced the cause of the oppressed and marginalized. Heine's life and work can be seen clearly in the tradition of a combination of the 'new' with a love of popular culture and folk-lore. Of course the 'new' at the time included mould breaking composers such as Ludwig Beethoven who has now been appropriated by elements within the Establishment. The 'novel' was developing into a revolutionary art form challenging the courtly literature of medieval time. The young Heine was caught up in this cauldron. However two unrequited loves who haunted him throughout his life, both were cousins: Amalie and Therese. In poems such as: *'allnachtlich im traume'* he expresses the intensity of his emotions: raw and spontaneous. Here is the first verse translated into a popular version by the Marxist Hal Draper:

'Nightly I hear you in dreams – you speak

With kindness sincerest

I throw myself, weeping aloud and weak

At your sweet feet, my dearest.'

- Heine

Many have known these emotions, indeed some the acts themselves when intoxicated by love. This was published in a collection called: *'Book of Songs'* in 1827. Around this time, perhaps heart-broken, and certainly by politically motivation an atmosphere of cynicism combined by a mockery of authority becomes apparent and will continue in much of his work. Six years earlier the 'move' to the political was becoming apparent in his play-writing, in *'Almansor'* the servant of the protagonist comments at a public book burning ceremony:

'This was only a prelude; where they burn books they will eventually burn people'.

- Heine

This was certainly a portent of things to come, especially from the pen of a German Jew. Heine's work is rooted in the socio-political, it has its foundation in material reality but clearly transcends the 'mechanistic materialism' which was the 'ideology' of the rising bourgeois, and their world was the triumph of the machine. Engels states without equivocation:

'The materialism of the last (18th) century was primary mechanistic.'

- Engels. *'Feuerbach and the rise of Classical German Philosophy'.*

Heine's work doesn't exist in a dimension of 'abstractions' (Idealism), it does not tell fairy-stories which are told outside of history. Neither can his writing be understood within a worldview which works like a giant clock sprung into motion by a First Cause and in constant motion until it somehow achieves ultimate perfection, a concept derived originally from Aristotle and integrated into Christian theology by Thomas Aquinas. Equally he goes beyond a world only experienced robotically by sensual experience as described by John Locke. His work is sensual yet transcendent and has the resonance which is, to employ a phrase of the Marxist critic Walter Benjamin, 'free, spontaneous utterance of the creature' as in the poem:

Desperately Seeking...

> *'God knows where that crazy woman's*
>
> *Found herself a place to stay;*
>
> *I've been looking for her in this*
>
> *Cursed rain for half the day'.*

- Heine

He required a revolutionary perspective in which to articulate his innovations. He would become aware of this as a consequence of leaving Germany in 1831.Heine moved to France where he would spend the rest of his life. Here he would meet people like the feminist writer and revolutionary George Sand.

It was during these early years in Paris that Heine met Karl Marx and mixed with a Utopian socialist group, the Saint-Simonists, these were pivotal moments. Heine would never embrace the fully articulated system created by Marx and Engels; 'Scientific Socialism' but he was writing for the young Marx's weekly journal *'Vorwarts'* in the early 1830's. He writing now developed a clear revolutionary socialist tone with poems such as *The Weavers Song'* which was about an insurrection of weavers in 1844:

> *'From darkened eyes no tears are falling*
>
> *With gritted teeth we sit here calling*
>
> *Germany, listen, ere we disperse,*
>
> *We weave your shroud with a triple curse*
>
> *We weave we are weaving.*

> - Heine

This was written in the same year as Marx wrote his great study of 'alienation' and 'struggle': *Economic and Philosophical Manuscripts'*. Heine also caught the revolutionary consciousness inherent in the proletariat. As with all utopian socialists, which often draw on a 'primitive Christianity' Heine didn't understand the inevitable consequence of the rise of capitalism was a working class revolution which would create more for the majority in a higher synthesis both materially and culturally. Rather he tended to see socialism as a kind of sensual monastic community. Nevertheless Marx was an admirer of Heinz's work and maintained a close friendship as his daughter Eleanor Marx wrote:

'He loved him just as much as his works,
and was as indulgent as can be towards
his political weaknesses. Poets, he declared,
are peculiar people. You cannot measure them
with the usual scale for normal people'.

— Eleanor Marx: *Neue Zeit*

Heine's poem *'Germany: A Winter's Tale'* provides us with a vision of the future:

'A new song, a better song,
oh friends I'll sing for you.
here on earth we mean to make
our paradise comes true.
we mean to be happy here on earth.

— Heine

Heinrich Heine was both a great Romantic poet and a revolutionary writer. His flaw was an inability to differentiate the utopian from the authentic revolutionary traditions, a poet of his times and still an inspiration to the oppressed today.

On the revolutionary poetry of Bertolt Brecht

'The poet has watched the people's mouth.'
                                        - Bertolt Brecht

Bertolt Brecht is probably best known for his
experimental plays and the dramatic theory he
developed around them. But he was also one of the
most important poets of the 20th century and arguably
the most significant Marxist poet of this epoch, he wrote
1,500 poems. But he also entered into debates over the
nature of 'Socialist Realism', which he deplored, with
Lukcas in the 1920s/30s, a polemic which divided
Marxist aesthetics into the 1960's and beyond.
Therefore this analysis will address these issues: 1)
what were the conditions and circumstances that
moulded Brecht's creative work and aesthetics 2) the
debate between Brecht and Lukcas on the nature of
socialist writing 3) the content and nature of Brecht's
Marxist poetry and 4) Brecht's great error of not actively
supporting a worker's uprising in East Berlin in 1953
which was crushed by Russian military power and his
subsequent withdrawal from the field of Marxist poetry
and aesthetics and 6) Brecht's impact on the
Situationist International.

Brecht was born in 1898 and would therefore
experience all the major events which shaped the 20th
century until 1956. Of course the first crisis was the First
World War which Lenin had correctly analysed as the
result of competing Capitals exporting 'finance capital' in
an attempt to stabilize and expand their own capitalist
economies and the inevitable conflict which would
ensue i.e. World War 1. Brecht was a military orderly
towards the end of the war and this experience of

imperialist war and its bloody results were an important developmental factor for the young Brecht. No longer would the tradition of Goethe and Romanticism dominate German literature; the world had been objectively changed. An early poem by Brecht captures his horror of and the hypocrisy of the war (Brecht had not had access to Marxist of Leninist writing at this time) called:

'The Legend of the Dead soldier'

'And when the war was four springs old

And of peace there was not a breath

The soldier took the logical step

And died a hero's death.

The war however was not yet done

So the Kaiser was displeased to be sure

That the soldier had given up like that

To him it seemed premature.

The soldier is then dug up and pronounced fit for active service. Accompanied by an army Chaplin and draped in a German flag he is escorted through cheering crowds on his way back to the front line.

So many were dancing around him now
That the soldier could hardly be seen
You could only see him from the sky above
And there only stars can gleam

...

The stars are not forever there.
Daylight gives new breath.'

— Bertolt Brecht

The next significant stage was Brecht being introduced,
by two women who were both committed communists
and also lovers of Brecht named Helene Weigel and
Elisabeth Hauptmann, too classical Marxist texts.
Hauptmann noted in her workbook on 25th October
1926:

> '*Brecht obtains works on socialism and*
> *Marxism and asks for lists of the basic*
> *works to study first.'*

— Elisabeth Hauptmann

By 1929 and the Wall Street Crash which was followed
by the Great Depression of the 1930's Brecht had
studied Marxist economics and philosophy, some Lenin
and early Mao Tse-tung on dialectics and the role of the
artist in the revolutionary struggle. But fascism was on
the rise throughout Europe; now Brecht was
ideologically prepared for it and in this poem delineates
what he believed should be the attitude of the poet
towards it:

> '*Within me here is a conflict between delight in*
> *the blooming apple-tree*
> *And the horror of the painter's* speeches.*
> *But only the second*
> *Drives me to my desk.'*

— Bertolt Brecht

*Brecht always referred to Hitler as 'the painter' because
he had been a house painter.

Therefore it is possible to discern four elements in the formation of Brecht's poetry: 1) imperialist war, 2) embracing Marxism as a world-view, 3) the inevitable decline of capitalism and 4) the rise of fascism. His aesthetic was rooted in the class-struggle; you can perceive his use of everyday language and form. Brecht's position became:

> '*For art to become "unpolitical" means only*
> *to ally itself with the 'ruling group"*
>
>   - Bertolt Brecht

However during this period there was a debate within Marxism regarding the correct 'line' on literature. Lukcas argued, in the 1920/30's, that 19th century realist novels reveal the true horrors of capitalism with 'typical' characters, hence the need for 'socialist realist' novels. Brecht disagreed and argued that the 19th century realist form is outdated and has no capacity to radicalize the oppressed and that new 'dialectical' forms were necessary. He argued in the 1930's against those who pursued the official Moscow 'line' of socialist realism:

'*They are, to put it bluntly, enemies of production[14].*
Production makes them feel uncomfortable. You never
know where you are with production; production is
unforeseeable. you never know what's going to come
out. And they themselves don't want to produce.
They want to play the apparatchik[15]and exercise control
over other people.'

                   - Bertolt Brecht

---

[14]For Brecht all 'production' is artistic 'production', a free 'collective act' (Brecht)
[15]Apparatchik: Communist Party functionary in the former Soviet Union.

Marx and Engels were against 'applied tendency' in literature and Marx described it as:

'*The most wretched offal of socialist literature.*'

- Karl Marx

Brecht used everyday language in his poetry but he poses a dialectical question, it demands a response. In the poem: 'The Sixteen-Year Old Seamstress Emma Ries before the Magistrate' Brecht exhibits two essential aspects of his poetry; 1) that it is worker centered and 2) that it incorporates a knowledge and application of Dialectical Materialism, the science of the proletariat. The poem is about a sixteen year old working class woman who has been caught distributing revolutionary leaflets. She is in a material situation, not in the vacuous spheres of bourgeois speculation. It is also the inevitable dialectical situation workers are objectively drawn into...she is in conflict with the oppressors. So here is the dialectical contradiction and how Brecht does resolve this contradiction, of course in the same manner the working class must ultimately resolve it, by revolutionary synthesis:

'*As reply, she stood up and sang*
the Internationale
When the magistrate shook his head
She shouted: 'Stand up! This
is the Internationale!'

- Bertolt Brecht

Therefore it is clear that in his poetry Brecht is creating a new tradition in German poetry, moving away from the themes and methods of Goethe and the Romantics and towards the future of communism.

However once ensconced in the German Democratic Republic in the role of Staatsdicher (state poet), a role he was never comfortable in Brecht made the biggest mistake of his life. It was 1953 and a spontaneous workers uprising erupted in East Berlin, after hesitation he finally supported the Stalinist elite in calling for Russian tanks to crush the revolt. He never recovered from this error and retreated into rustic silence and a poetic wasteland. But Brecht was not entirely curbed by this error and in the aftermath of the rebellion wrote one of his best anti-Stalinist/anti-capitalist poems:

> *'The Solution.'*
> *...Would it not be easier*
> *In that case for the government*
> *To dissolve the people*
> *And elect another.'*
>
> - Bertolt Brecht

Finally I would like to examine the relationship between Brecht and the Situationalist International's concept of detournement 'anything can be used' (Guy Debord) to disrupt the alienation within the 'Society of the Spectacle.' To put it more abruptly: 'Plagiarism is necessary. Progress implies it.' (Debord). It is necessary to place this in the context that for the Situationalists art was concluded when the Spartacus League failed to bring German dada to fruition in the workers revolution of 1919. They reflected with pleasure that Brecht had commented:

> *'That he had made some cuts in the classics of theatre in order to make the performances more educative...close to the revolutionary orientation we are calling for.'*
>
> - Debord/Wolman

Brecht encapsulates his aesthetic in the poem:

> '*Hymn to Communism*'.
> '*It is so simple which is so difficult.*'

- Bertolt Brecht

The life and ideas of Emma Goldman

Emma Goldman was a woman who defied those who would oppress humanity generally and her specific contribution to the rise of revolutionary feminism is today of major significance. Her refusal to submit to the jackboot of any ideology she regarded as tyrannical, whether it was American capitalism or what she regarded as mistakes made by the Russian Marxists around the Kronstadt uprising in 1921, is an inspiration to the downtrodden masses today . But revolutionaries never grow old and as a mature woman of 67 she traveled to Spain in 1936 to help organize the defense of the revolution against the fascists and other agents of international Capital. She was both a theoretician and an activist who wrote some of the most important documents of modern anarchism and also spent time in prison because of her refusal to be silenced.

Emma was born into a Jewish family living in Lithuania in 1869. But because of the backlash from the state after the assassination of Tsar Alexander 11 in 1881, there was great political oppression and pogroms against Jews, the family moved to St.Petersberg when Emma was 13. As a consequence of their economic hardship she had to leave school after six months and work in a textiles factory. It was here that Emma was introduced to revolutionary ideas and read a novel by Nikolai Chernyshevsky called: What is to be Done in which the heroine Vera becomes a nihilist and lives in a world where there is not any hierarchy in gender relationships and where all work is done on a co-operative basis. These experiences, both emotional and intellectual, would create within Emma a distrust of state authority and a desire for freedom, they created the foundations on which her anarchist politics and philosophy would later be constructed. In 1931 she encapsulated her beliefs succinctly:

> "*I want freedom, the right to self-expression, everyone's right to beautiful, radiant things*".
>
> - Emma Goldman

By the age of 15 Emma was becoming a lively young woman, her father's response was to get her married, she refused and consequently her parents decided to send her to America. Emma soon realized that the U.S.A. was not the land of opportunity for the masses, but a capitalist system based on exploitation. She married a fellow factory worker and gained U.S. citizenship. Would her life be worn down into dust by capitalist oppression and patriarchy domination? At the age of 20 things were rather bleak, but in 1886 something occurred which would again ignite the fire within Emma. The anarchist movement in the U.S. was quite active at this time and during a clash between militant workers and the police in Chicago, the workers were demanding an eight-hour day, someone threw a bomb into a group of police. Eight anarchists were convicted on very flimsy evidence; the judge even told them they were on trail "because you are anarchists". Four anarchist comrades were hung and became known in working-class history as the Haymarket Martyrs. On the day of the verdict Emma decided to become a revolutionary. Her marriage had not been a success so Emma now divorced her husband, moved to New York and joined the community of anarchist thinkers and activists. Emma was realizing that:

> "*It requires less mental energy to condemn than to think*".
>
> - Emma Goldman

She was thinking and contemplating action:

Having traced Emma Goldman's early years to the point where she embraced revolutionary anarchism I would now like to examine four areas of her thought:

1) Her commitment to the concept of "propaganda by deed" which had been developed by the anarchist thinker and activist Mikhail Bakunin.

2) Emma's analysis of religion and the failure of Christianity.

3) Goldman and the Bolsheviks.

4) Her ideas on the nature of love.

Emma was initially attracted to anarchists of the Bakuninite tendency who were, in the U.S., grouped around Johann Most. She embraced many of Mikhail Bakunin's ideas because he had argued that anarchism was the:

> "*absolute rejection of every authority including that which sacrifices freedom for the convenience of the state.*"
>
> -Mikhail Bakunin

The position he was arguing for here would not be considered particularly militant in revolutionary circles and formed a basic tenet of anarchist philosophy. However Bakunin's ideas of how to achieve the raising of the consciousness of the oppressed from that of their day to day struggles to that of revolutionary action were radical and are still contested by some anarchists and many Marxists in the anti-capitalist movement today, he argued that:

"*we must spread our principles, not with words but with*

deeds, for this is the most popular, the most potent, and the most irresistible form of propaganda."
- Mikhail Bakunin

This theory was called "propaganda by deed", it was assumed that a revolutionary act, often of individual violence, would arouse the masses to take place in an insurrection and overthrow the existing order. This was an essential component of Bakunin's political philosophy. He followed this argument to its logical conclusion and perceived the revolutionary's emotions of hostility towards the system as a manifestation of creativity:

"The passion for destruction is a creative passion".

- Mikhail Bakunin

The reason Bakunin's position is criticized by most Marxist revolutionaries is because it detaches an individual activist from the collective nature of working class struggle. These comrades argue that revolutionaries should organize themselves in a revolutionary party within the most advanced sections of the working class and when historical necessity creates the circumstances this "vanguard" should intervene in a decisive way. This party of organized activists will, it is argued, play a leading role in guiding the proletariat towards its "world historic task" (Engels) of creating the "dictatorship of the proletariat", which is the rule of the majority. Once created a "workers state" will, as objective conditions allow, "wither away" (Engels) to leave a classless society.

Both anarchists and Marxists believe that the creation of a society without class or gender hierarchies is the desirable conclusion of social transformation.

Nevertheless Emma was, at this time, convinced of the truth of Bakunin's theory of "propaganda by deed". While in New York she met Alexander Berkman, a friend of Johann Most and follower of Bakunin, Emma and Alexander became lovers and would remain life-long friends. This core of three intellectuals was committed to the idea of "propaganda by deed". Goldman and Berkman closely followed a violent strike taking place in 1912 known as the 'Homestead Strike'. The workers had occupied the factory but were expelled by gunmen hired by the owners, several workers died in the struggle. Emma and Alexander were enraged; Goldman gives an account of their feelings (Frick was the manager):

"We were stunned. We saw at once that the time for our manifesto had passed. Words had lost their meaning in the face of innocent blood spilled. Intuitively each felt what was surging in the heart of the other. Sasha [Alexander Berkman] broke the silence. "Frick is the responsible factor in this crime," he said; "he must be made to stand the consequences." It was the psychological moment for an Attentat (i.e., assassination); the whole country was aroused, everybody was considering Frick the perpetrator of a coldblooded murder. A blow aimed at Frick would re-echo in the poorest hovel, would call the attention of the whole world to the real cause behind the Homestead struggle. It would also strike terror in the enemy's ranks and make them realize that the proletariat of America had its avengers".

-Emma Goldman

Emma then tried, unsuccessfully, to prostitute herself to raise money to buy a gun, but eventually Berkman carried out an unsuccessful assignation attempt for which he was sent to prison for 22 years, being released on parole after 14 years. Berkman had refused to implicate Emma in the action and she campaigned for his release. Johann Most, who had been at the heart of the Bakuninite movement in the U.S., suddenly changed his position, condemned Berkman in his newspaper and accused him of creating sympathy for Flick.

Emma continued with her political activities, but was disillusioned with the Bakuninite tactic of "propaganda by deed". She remained an active agitator and shared platforms with the I.W.W. (International Workers of the World) that were an anarcho-syndicalist organization committed to working class struggle. In 1916 Emma was arrested for her feminist activities, she was distributing radical literature to women workers

We can see how Emma's Bakuninite tendencies lead her to make errors in the tactics to be employed by revolutionaries. But her refusal to be gagged by the State, patriarchy or capitalist oppression is something which can be admired today.

Next I would like to examine Emma Goldman's ideas about Atheism and Christianity. Her ideas were fine tuned 1913-16. She was to a considerable degree influenced by Fredrick Nietzsche who she described as a "great mind". His proclamation that "God was dead" resounded through the world of all thinking people in the modern period. For Nietzsche the problem was once there is not a Divine "first cause" or Creator God for Nature then everything is in chaos. How can human beings live authentically in these circumstances? A part of his answer was derived from his reading of Schopenhauer and the concepts of "appearance" and "reality". Nietzsche applied these concepts to Greek culture: the Apollonian seen as the intellectualizing, the world of "appearances", and the Dionysian as the wild and stormy dimension which is tuned into real life or "reality", the "will-to-life", the creative.

It was this "will-to life" that Nietzsche and Goldman believed was being suppressed by Christianity and religion in general. Emma said:

> "*The Atheists know that life is not fixed,*
> *but fluctuating, even as life itself is*".

> - Emma Goldman

This is her recognition of the life-force, the Dionysian as opposed to Apollonian. That is not to suggest that Goldman was not an intellectual, for she most certainly was, but that she was in touch with the essence of life itself. An illustration of this occurred on an occasion when Emma was dancing and a young comrade took her to one side and said that this was not correct behavior for an agitator, Emma replied:

"*Our cause should not expect me to behave*
like a nun, the movement should not be turned
into a cloister, if it means that, I do not want it".
> - Emma Goldman

Of Nietzsche she said:

"*Nietzsche was not a social theorist, but a poet,*
a rebel and innovator. His aristocracy was neither
of birth or purse; it was of the spirit. In this respect
Nietzsche was an anarchist".
> - Emma Goldman

Her views on political violence underwent a further transformation whilst she was in revolutionary Russia in the early 1920s. Goldman had advocated "propaganda by deed", but had renounced it after the debacle of 1912. However after that period Emma was still in favour of "defensive" working class violence. In revolutionary Russia, she came to the conclusion that the Bolsheviks had institutionalized political violence and terrorism. Her analysis was:

> "*Such terrorism begets counter-revolution and in turn becomes counter-revolutionary*".
> - Emma Goldman

However she wrote to Berkman in 1926 that there was only one choice open to people: either to become a Bolshevik or a Tolstoy an (Tolstoy had theorized the "Holy Peasant" as the basic unit of the agrarian anarchy-pacifist commune). Tolstoy had said:

"There is only one permanent revolution and that is a moral one: the regeneration of the inner man".
> - Leo Tolstoy

Emma was once asked about her ideas on "free love", she replied:

"Free love? As if love is anything but free! Love is free; it can dwell in no other atmosphere".

> - Emma Goldman

She went on to define her"free love":

"My love is sex, but it is devotion, care, patience, friendship, it is all."
> - Emma Goldman

Breaking the chains: creativity and recovery

*'Many of the most sincerest and gifted
artists and writers in this capitalist world
are conscious of a loss of reality.'*

- Ernst Fischer: 'The Necessity of Art'

Some theorists of language, such as the 'Russian Formalists' have argued that this 'loss of reality' is a positive aspect to writing and the processes of language generally. The 'Formalists' existed before the revolution of October 1917 in Russia and thrived in the creativity of the post-revolutionary period of the 1920's, only to be crushed by the counter-revolutionary Stalinists during the 1930's. They moved attention away from the symbolist interpretation of literature to a more material approach to the text. What is of interest to us about them is the 'concept' of the 'defamaliarizating effect' or what they called 'making strange'. The first step of their argument is that literature is condensed by Jan Mukarosky:

> *'In the maximum of the foregrounding of the utterance, that is bring the act of expression to the foreground, into prominence for the reader.'*

- Mukarosky

The concept of foregrounding therefore is to put the 'linguistic medium' i.e. literature at the front of our perceptions. Victor Shklovsky argues this creates estrangement or a defamaliarizating effect, by disrupting the everyday uses of language literature 'makes strange' the world of everyday life a and renews the readers lost capacity for a new experience; essentially literature disrupts the 'mundane' which is part of our experience of alienation under capitalism. Therefore it is possible to argue that a 'loss of reality' or even the process of 'making strange' can be understood as positive elements in writing.

Having established the idiosyncratic nature of 'authentic' writing I will now construct a model of consciousness and language as formed by Marx and Engels which will then be developed by the philosophy of language created by Valentine Voloshinov in the late 1920's. Then this model will be applied to the journey taken by Jean-Paul Sartre from his first novel of 1938: 'Nausea' which is a work of existential dread and horror which expresses the essence of Sartre's existentialism to his crowning philosophical text: 'Critique of Dialectical Reason' which offers a path to freedom through 'praxis' from the existential anguish of his early novel.

Firstly then how did Marx and Engels conceptualize and therefore understand the categories of and the relationship between consciousness and language? The response is multi-dimensional to quote Terry Eagleton:

> '*Turned the whole history of philosophy of humanity on its head, revolutionized it with the statement: 'my method is movement upwards from the abstract to the concrete.'*

- Eagleton

This is the foundation for the overarching thesis I present here i.e. Historical and Dialectical Materialism. For Marx and Engels we live in a material world. b) The material source of consciousness is material:

> '*Thought and consciousness are products of the human brain.*'

- Engels

81

This may seem obvious, but for many people the source of awareness is not the brain but 'The Idea' (Hegel), a 'First Cause' (Aristotle) or a 'Supreme Being' (Thomas Aquinas). So what is the nature of this 'consciousness' described by Engels?

> *'First came labour; after it, and then side by side with it, articulate speech.'*

- Engels

This process is social and the result of people not only interacting with their environment but each other:

> *'in order to produce they enter into definite connections and relations with one another, and within these social connections and relations do their activity take place.'*

- Marx

Therefore labour and language are social in nature. This position is developed further:

'First labour, then articulate speech was the two main stimuli under the influence of which the brain of the ape gradually changed into the human brain. The development of labour brought the members of the community more closely together...these relations gave rise to the need for primitive man to speak and communicate with each other.'

- Schneierson

Here, therefore, is the fundamental model on which this thesis is constructed upon.

Now I will look at two models of language in the light of the model constructed above. First, Ferdinand de Saussure in his 'Course of General Linguistics'(1913) created a theory which would influence all following study of language. It consisted of:

a) There exists a pre-established or ahistorical structure of language before its realization as writing and speech.

b) It consisted of chains of 'signs'. Each 'sign' is made up of 1) Signifier which is the sound or written image of 2) the Signified or meaning/concept. e.g. in English the signifier't r e e' is related to the signified Tree and therefore creates the word TREE. But this is random because in other languages the signified tree would have a different signifier...

Because for Saussure this structure is detached from socio-history it is profoundly opposed to Marxism, but a Russian Marxist linguist named Valentine Voloshinov took it up in a study called 'Marxism and the Study of Language' (1929). He accepted the concept of the 'sign':

> *'The entire reality of a word is absorbed in being a 'sign'.*
>
> - Voloshinov

However ideology which here means both ideas and 'false consciousness' (Marx) is transmitted through language:

> *'everything ideological possesses semiotic (sign) value'.*
>
> - ibid

So for Voloshinov the false dichotomy between the material base and ideological superstructure of classical Marxism is resolved through language or 'signs'. However he recognizes the limitations of the 'sign'

'Signs only arise...they become material only socially, they comprise a group and only then do they take (real) shape.'

-ibid

But it is when 'sign' or words become what Saussure had called 'parole' or 'utterances' that they become significant i.e. both material and socially interactive. Language is as Engels had argued a defining human characteristic. Voloshinov enhances this position:

'In point of fact, the word is a two-sided act. It is determined equally by whose word it is and for whom it is meant.'

The 'word' therefore introduces not monologue but dialogue...we communicate with others, he concludes:

'A word is the product of the reciprocal relationship between speaker and listener. Each and every word the 'one in relation to the other.'

- ibid

I would now like to apply this theoretical construct to the journey taken by Jean-Paul Sartre from the existentialist 'dread' of his novel 'Nausea'(1938) to the concept of 'praxis' as a path to freedom in 'Critique of Dialectical Reason'(1960). A path through human creativity as social rather than merely individual which can be seen as the solution to 'absurdity' characterized as mental health issues. The central character in 'Nausea' says;

'The nausea has not left me; I think it will be some time before it does...it is no longer an illness or a passing fit: it is I.'

- Sartre (1938)

The words nausea or sickness appear in two other of Sartre's works; 1) 'The Psychology of the Imagination' (1940) 'are conscious of a nauseating sickness.' and 2) in his first major philosophical work 'Being and Nothingness' (1943) 'dullness...feeling of sickness.' Why? Sartre defines three modes of being a) 'Being-in-itself' this are objects which simply exist like a tree, b) 'Being-for-itself' this is humanity, because we have no pre-determined essence, there is no 'First Cause', for Sartre, we make ourselves, we create ourselves. It is the absurd contrast between these two forms of being which is one cause for Nausea, c)'Being-for-Others', here Sartre says we only become aware of our 'being' when in the 'gaze' of another, when someone 'looks' at you. Thus:

> '*I find myself in a state of instability in relation to the Other.*'
>
> *- Sartre (1943)*

This is where Sartre's infamous phrase 'Hell is other people' is derived from. Any belief in a system of ideas or faith was, according to Sartre at this time, 'bad faith'.

But Sartre discovered the analytical tools provided by Marx and Engels and renewed them in order to explain and transcend this existential dread or 'Nausea' in 'Critique of Dialectical Reason': 1) he embraced Marx's concept of conscious human activity as the dynamic of History, once this was established he had to explain his early position of 'Nausea', 2) in order to achieve this Sartre created the idea of the 'Practico-inert' which is when humans are active but not social like atoms whirling around in a system and 3) he provided the solution of 'praxis' or 'depasssement' (going beyond the existing situation). This is a refinement of Marx's concept of 'species-being' which was, he said, the essence of humans i.e. to act interact with the world and each other. For Sartre 'praxis' and 'activity' are at the heart of the solution. This 'praxis' is genuine social activity created and made two-way by language:

'We set off from the immediate, that is to say the individual fulfilling him/herself to the totality of bonds with others...absolute concrete people.'

- Sartre (1960)

The social is creative and the creative is social, they are only divided in a social system which has what Marx called the 'division of labour' between mental and manual labour and ultimately between those who are compelled to sell 'social labour', which is their creativity, and to those who buy and profit from it.

But the only way to prevent the commoditization of art is to abolish commodity capitalism; one is dependent on the other. But maintaining an active dialogue between artists and writers is a key step in breaking the chains of mental ill health and aiding recovery.

The life and poetry of Vladimir Mayakovsky

Vladimir Mayakovsky was a great poet who challenged conventions both in the world of poetry and in the social sphere. For many of those of us who see the workers revolution in Russia of October 1917 as the pinnacle of human endeavour and within its theory the foundations for future human attainment it, therefore, follows that as the most significant poet of the Russian insurrectionary masses of October 1917 Mayakovsky represents the highest level of achievement in modern poetry. Leon Trotsky wrote in his study of revolutionary writing, 'Literature and Revolution' that proletarian poets like Mayakovsky:

> *"(Have to) reshape the world of feelings.*
> *Not everybody is capable of it. That is why there*
> *are many people in this world that think as*
> *revolutionaries and feel as Philistines."*

- Leon Trotsky

His artistic talents were not, however, confined to poetry; he designed book coversas well as Agitprop posters and, also drew.

Mayakovsky was born in Russia in 1893. After the premature death of his father the family moved to Moscow, here his elder sister Lyudmila became a student and was radicalized by Marxists. She brought home socialist literature, both legal and illegal and Vladimir was set on fire, intellectually and emotionally, by this material. At the age of 14 he joined the Bolshevik Party. In 1908 he was arrested for possession of revolutionary proclamations, he was placed on probation. Later during the same year Mayakovsky was enrolled in the Moscow Art School, it was while a student there that he became aware of the Futurist movement. Vladimir was arrested again in 1909 for political activism. A report written by one of the wardens confirmed his revolutionary credentials:

> "*Vladimir Mayakovsky by his behavior*
> *incites the other prisoners to disobedience*
> *towards prison wardens.......purporting to*
> *be the prisoner's spokesman.*"

He was moved around the prison system and eventually placed in solitary confinement; it was whilst in "solitary" that he wrote his first poem. By 1912 Mayakovsky was out of prison and in the December of that year published a Futurist Manifesto called: 'A Slap in the Face of Public Taste', this is reproduced below:

A Slap in the Face of Public Taste

To the readers of our New First Unexpected.

We alone were the face of our Time. Through us the horn of time blows in the art of the world.

The past is too tight. The Academy and Pushkin are less intelligible than hieroglyphics.

Throw Pushkin, Dostoevsky, Tolstoy, etc., etc. overboard from the Ship of Modernity.

He who does not forget his first love will not recognize his last.

Who, trustingly, would turn his last love toward Balmont's perfumed lechery? Is this the reflection of today's virile soul?

Who, faint-heartedly, would fear tearing from warrior Bryusov's black tuxedo the paper armor-plate? Or does the dawn of unknown beauties shine from it?

Wash your hands which have touched the filthy slime of the books written by the countless Leonid Andreyevs.

All those Maxim Gorkys, Krupins, Bloks, Sologubs, Remizovs, Averchenkos, Chornys, Kuzmins, Bunins, etc. need only a dacha on the river. Such is the reward fate gives tailors.

From the heights of skyscrapers we gaze at their insignificance!

We order that the poets' rights be revered:

- *To enlarge the scope of the poet's vocabulary with arbitrary and derivative words (Word-novelty).*
- *To feel an insurmountable hatred for the language existing before their time.*
- *To push with horror off their proud brow the Wreath of cheap fame that You have made from bathhouse switches.*
- *To stand on the rock of the word "we" amidst the sea of boos and outrage.*

And if for the time being the filthy stigmas of your "common sense" and "good taste" are still present in our lines, these same lines for the first time already glimmer with the Summer Lightning of the New Coming Beauty of the Self-sufficient (self-centered) Word.

~ David Burliuk, Alexander Kruchenykh, Vladmir Mayakovsky, Victor Khlebnikov

Their manifesto was an outcry against the literary establishment, a celebration of the new in art and poetry and an attack on so-called common sense. Russian Futurism was opposed to all forms of deification whether by the Romantic poets of Nature or any other form of mysticism. They believed in breaking the mould and saw in the rhythms of the machine and the throbbing of the oppressed masses a new style for both poetry and society. Essentially Mayakovsky and his fellow poets and artists believed in removing the artificial boundary between art and everyday life which had been created by the bourgeois culture. They would travel around Russia and perform spontaneous shows of poetry, drama and art in the way that would be repeated during the1960's, when another movement of radical ideas in the arena of art and politics would arise; these impromptu art events were called "happenings". Also in 1912 his first poems were published.

Icarus Still Flies

By 1914 the old political radicalism had returned to Mayakovsky and because of this he was expelled from the Moscow Art School. That year his first long poem: 'A Cloud in Trousers' was published, it is very significant because of the combination of its themes of revolution, love art and religion from the perspective of a rejected lover. However its most important contribution to modern literature is that Mayakovsky used the language of the street:

"Your thoughts,
dreaming on a softened brain,
like an over-fed lackey on a greasy settee,
with my heart's bloody tatters I'll mock again;
impudent and caustic, I'll jeer to superfluity.

Of Grandfatherly gentleness I'm devoid,
there's not a single grey hair in my soul!
Thundering the world with the might of my voice,
I go by -- handsome,
twenty-two-year-old.

If you like-
I'll be furiously flesh elemental,
or - changing to tones that the sunset arouses -
if you like-
I'll be extraordinary gentle,
not a man, but - a cloud in trousers!"

(he continues arguing that the poverty-stricken and labour exhausted outcasts will slowly become aware of their moral superiority over the corrupt and decaying capitalist world):

"I know, the sun would fade out, almost,
stunned by our souls Hellenic beauty".
                    - Mayakovsky

In the summer of 1915 Mayakovsky fell in love, it was to be the greatest love of his life, with Lilya Birk. She was married to Osip Brik who was his publisher, but despite her marriage Lilya fell in love with Mayakovsky.

Describing the evening they met Osip Brik said:

"His reading was fascinating. It was what we had been waiting for. We had not been able to read anything for some time. All poetry seemed worthless-- poets were writing not in the right way and not about the right things, and here suddenly were both."

When she told her husband that she'd fallen in love:

> *"all three of us decided never to part from one another."*
>
> - Lilya Birk

The Russian proletariat led by the Bolshevik Party seized power in the revolution of October 1917, this was only the second time the working class had overthrown the class oppression of capitalism, the other being the 'Paris Commune' of 1871. This revolt was the pivotal point in world History which is the History of class struggle and heralded in a new epoch for humanity. Lenin had maintained that in these circumstances:

"(poets and artists) are the cogs and wheels of the whole revolutionary machine."

> - Lenin

Mayakovsky was at the heart of the insurrection; indeed as 'Red' sailors stormed the 'Winter Palace' they chanted one of his slogans:

> *"Eat peaches, chew on quail*
> *Your last day is coming, bourgeois!"*

As the struggle to maintain and spread the revolution intensified Mayakovsky wrote one of his best known poems:

Left March

For the Red Marines: 1918

Rally the ranks into a march!
Now's no time to quibble or browse there.
Silence, you orators!
You
have the floor,
Comrade Mauser.
Enough of living by laws
that Adam and Eve have left.
Hustle old history's horse.
LEFT!
LEFT!
LEFT!

Ahoy, blue jackets!
Cross the sky-moats!
Beyond the oceans!
Unless
your battleships on the roads
blunted their keels' fighting keenness!
Baring the teeth of his crown,
let
the lion of Britain whine, gale-heft.
The commune can never go down.
LEFT!
LEFT!
LEFT!

There-
beyond sorrow's peaks,
sunlit lands uncharted.
Against hunger,

against plague's dark seas,
the marching of millions has started!
Let armies of hirelings ambush us,
streaming cold steel through every rift, -
L'Entente can't conquer the Russians,
LEFT!
LEFT!
LEFT!

Does the eye of the eagle fade?
Shall we stare back to the old?
Proletarian fingers
the throat of the world
still tighter hold!
Chests out!
Shoulders straight!
Stick to the sky red flags adrift!
Whose marching there with the right?!!
LEFT!
LEFT!
LEFT!

- Mayakovsky

The link between the aesthetic and bohemian revolt of
the leftist Futurists and the revolutionary Marxist poet-
revolutionaries is clear. Mayakovsky and his circle were
from a disaffected and untamed segment of the left
intelligentsia which refused to be incorporated into the
bourgeoisie and, therefore, into capitalism. In other
words they didn't "sell-out". Their orientation could,
hence, only be towards the exploited and downtrodden
masses and the role of leading them in a revolutionary
struggle. Mayakovsky's development as a human being,
a poet and a revolutionary, was therefore profoundly
connected to the fate of the Russian Revolution. The
years 1922-1928 saw him as a leading member of the
'Left Art Front' which was active in spreading the

revolution. At this time he was defining his work as "Communist Futurism". As the betrayal of the revolution by the Stalinist reactionaries that took place after the death of Lenin, this had its material foundations in the inability of the 'Union of Soviet Socialist Republics' (the Workers State) to spread its revolution internationally, the gains of the 1917 revolution were being rolled back. As a result Mayakovsky began to decline artistically and emotionally. He was being constrained by a system which had heralded the dawn of human freedom, but was now acting against the interests of the masses. In 1929 he was compelled to join the bureaucratically controlled 'Soviet Association of Proletarian Poets'. The same year he fell in love with Tatiana Yakovleva, but sadly this relationship wasn't to be successful. The failure of the revolution combined with sadness in love was too much for him, on the evening of April 14th 1930 Mayakovsky committed suicide by shooting himself. He eloquently describes his inner contradictions:

'On the Top of my Voice'

Agitprop
            sticks
                        in my teeth too,
and I'd rather
                  compose
                              romances for you--
more profit in it
                  and more charm
But I
        subdued
                    myself,
                              setting my heel

on the throat
                  of my own song.
Listen, comrades of prosperity,
to the agitator, the rabble-rouser.
Stifling the torrents of poetry,
I'll skip the volumes of lyrics;
as one alive, I'll address the living.
I'll join you in the far communist future.

- Mayakovsky

In an analysis of progressive writers the Marxist thinker
Leon Trotsky said:

*"(the poetry of Mayakovsky) was more bohemian than
proletarian"*

~ 'Leon Trotsky' (The Awkward Customer)

Victor Serge

Did the debates between Victor Serge and Leon Trotsky have answers for us today?

'Le Retif' (the Awkward Customer) was Victor Serge's first pseudonym in the early 1900's as a young man writing for an anarchist journal. Throughout his life he would challenge the conventional wisdom of whatever movement he was involved in from anarchism in Paris, Bolshevism in the USSR. (Russia) during the 1920/30's, questions about revolutionary Marxist strategy during the Spanish Civil War (in 1937) and finally opposition to Trotsky's founding of the 4th International in 1938 (note: an international group to organize world revolution which had its roots in the 1st International created by Karl Marx in 1864). Reverberations of his ideological positions effect revolutionaries and, indeed, anyone interested in social change today. This analysis will examine 1) Victor Serge's early live, 2) his involvement with Leon Trotsky in the anti-Stalinist 'Left Opposition' and 3) his break with Trotsky and the ensuing theoretical errors.

Firstly, Serge was born into a family of suspect revolutionary pedigree with his family involved around movement of the 'Narodnaya Volya' or 'People's Will' who assassinated Tsar Alexander 11 in 1881, an act which many Marxists opposed as Rosa Luxemburg pointed out:

> 'If one is willing to take a fitting label from the history of Western European socialism, then the term "Blanquist" would undoubtedly be the best description of the political strategy of the Narodnaya Volya. Blanquist is a strategy this is determined, on the one hand, to win the trust of the mass of the people, and on the other hand, to seize power by

means of a conspiratorial party which then institutes
only those parts of the socialist program "which are
possible."

- Rosa Luxemburg

Serge then went on to commit similar theoretical
mistakes, involving himself in groups of anarchist
organizations in France for which he was imprisoned for
alleged terrorist offences for five years 1912-17; he
wrote a fictional account of these experiences in the
novel: ' Men in Prison'(1930) . After being freed Serge
became an anarcho-syndicalist agitator in Barcelona, a
period he wrote about in the novel: 'Birth of our Power'
(1931) and finally after drawing the correct conclusions
from his formative errors he become a Bolshevik and
wrote another novel called 'Conquered City (1931)
about some of the hopes yet defeats in revolutionary
Petrograd between 1919-21 during the darkest days of
the civil war which followed the Russian Revolution of
October 1917.

The Bolsheviks had lead a successful workers
revolution in 1917, it was the highest moment of human
collective achievement and set the tone onwards...the
recent credit crunch and economic Depression have
brought Marxism and, therefore the nature and reasons
for the, ultimate, failure of the USSR back onto the
agenda. By 1921 the Workers State was in difficulties, it
had paid a high price for a bloody civil war with no less
than eighteen foreign armies assisting the 'counter-
revolutionary' forces. The astonishing bravery of the
'Red Army' lead by the genius of Leon Trotsky saved
the fledgling state, but at a large cost. The civil war had
been won, but the Soviet Union (Russia) was shaken, in
1920 Lenin argued that the USSR was a workers state
with bureaucratic deformations:

'Our Party Programme...shows that ours is a is a worker's state with a bureaucratic twist.'

- Lenin

These and other contradictions began to change the nature of the USSR. In the early 1920's a core of ideologically committed leftist Bolsheviks formed themselves into a group to oppose the degeneration of the revolution and the rising power of Stalin...by this time Lenin was ill and his influence waning. They called themselves the 'Left Opposition' and were lead by Trotsky. In 1923 Victor Serge, correctly, joined this group which was, at this point, a faction within the Communist Party.

Trotsky applied Marxist analysis to the situation within the Soviet Union and realized that a layer of the Communist Party had become a bureaucratic caste, but not a new ruling class, detached from the mass of workers. The reason Trotsky argued that they were not a ruling class was because although they had political power this did not extend to ownership of the 'means of production' (Marx) i.e. the economic base. Therefore Trotsky argued for a 'political revolution' to correct this 'Degenerated Workers State' which was his term to describe the Soviet Union from around the death of Lenin in 1924. This is the foundation of Trotskyist analysis of failed workers states although it has been developed by later followers of Trotsky, but most maintained his methodology.

However here was the root of Serge's second major theoretical error and deviation from Trotsky's towering analysis, he wrote in a pamphlet published in 1921:

> '*So it is that, even if State Communism deviates from its revolutionary and progressive orientation, it will have created the conditions...for a later evolution.*'

> - Victor Serge

Trotsky is arguing for revolution, Serge for evolution in post-revolutionary Russia.

This break with Trotsky was at the essence of all Serge's following theoretical and strategic mistakes. This particular mistake lead him to argue in 1935 against Trotsky that as the economy of the USSR was in an up-turn Stalin would introduce 'normalization' (the end of 'The Terror'), but 1936 saw one of the worst years of purges by the Stalinist ruling caste.

Another consequence of his inability to perceive the coherence and clarity of Trotsky's analysis of the true nature of Stalinism was Serge's uncritical support of the POUM leadership (the POUM were a party of dissident Marxists with anarcho-syndicalist sympathies who fought against both the fascists and the Stalinist forces during the Spanish Civil War). Trotsky supported the POUM in their struggle but, ultimately, as an instrument of proletarian revolution, he therefore placed the emphasis on the rank and file struggles. Serge, therefore, supported the entry of the POUM leadership into the Catalonian government in 1937 which effactually lead to the hopes of a successful workers and peasant's insurrection being crushed. Here is another example of Serge's inability to understand a key point of Trotskyist theory which is to build in the rank and file and not in a party (or trade-union) bureaucracy i.e. a detached leadership.

The result of his preceding inability to understand Trotsky's methodology lead him to oppose and vehemently criticize the creation of the 4th International by Trotsky in 1938 two years before the murder of the latter by a Stalinist agent. The essence of the 4th International was Trotsky's 'Transitional Programme':

'...it is necessary to begin by proclaiming a Programme that meets the needs of our epoch (late-capitalism). On the basis of this Programme it is necessary to mobilize co-thinkers, the pioneers of the new International. No other path is possible.'

- Leon Trotsky

Clearly an international revolutionary organization requires a Programme; not a wish-list but a guide to action and co-ordination.

The 2nd International (1884-1914) had set-out a 'minimalist' and 'maximalist' Programme. The minimalist demands were things like working hours and conditions etc. Demands which the capitalists would resist, but would not challenge the existence of the system. The 'maximalist' Programme called for social revolution, but was not linked to the minimal demands in a practical way. This contradiction allowed the right (minimalist)faction to dominate and the 2nd International collapsed on the eve of World War 1 with only two leading members voting against the war: Rosa Luxemburg and Lenin.

On the eve of the October 1917 Russian revolution Lenin wrote a pamphlet: 'The Impending Catastrophe and How to Combat It', as the masses prepared for insurrection he united the immediate demands of workers with revolutionary demands, the immediate needs of workers could only be met by seizing the private property of the rich and the masses seizing political power, therefore creating a 'bridge' between the old 'minimalist / maximalist' divide. This policy was used by the 3rd Communist International to influence the struggles of the global oppressed, but by the 6th Congress in 1928 Stalin and Bakunin reintroduced the same old divide.

Trotsky responded:

'The proletarian vanguard needs not a catalogue of truisms but a manual for action'.
- Leon Trotsky

Therefore in 1938 the 4th International created a Programme based on the actual situation facing the working-class at that time e.g. global economic depression, the rise of fascism and the proletariat's fight for global socialism. Hence the 4th International then made a number of 'transitional demands' to act as a 'bridge' between the everyday struggles of workers and their: 'world historic task' (Engels) which is to overthrow capitalism. Trotsky had studied in detail the history of the

International and concluded that the present period:

> *'Was characterized by a historical crisis of the leadership of the proletariat'.*

> - Leon Trotsky

He believed it was this failure that had saved capitalism through the crises years of the 1920-30's and had brought the world to the brink of fascist barbarianism, total economic collapse and war. The only solution was:

> *'A system of transitional demands, the essence of which is contained in the fact that ever more openly and decisive they will be directed against the very foundations of the bourgeois regime'.*

- Leon Trotsky

Although Trotsky was well aware of the limitations of trade-unions in the revolutionary struggle, on the basis of his method in 1938 he recommended participation in them:

> 'trade unions are not ends in themselves, they are but means along the road to the proletarian revolution.'
>
> - Leon Trotsky

Trotsky argued that a 'first step towards the socialist guidance of economic life' would be for key branches of industry and the banks to be taken out of the hands of private capitalists and placed under State control. However he makes abundantly clear that these gains:

> 'Produce favourable results only if state power passes completely from the hands of the exploiters into the hands of the toilers.'
>
> - Leon Trotsky

He addressed the nature of the tactics to be used against fascism which 'starts in the factory and ends in the streets' as opposed to the editorial room of a liberal newspaper. Trotsky argued that young workers active 'on picket-lines' should be recruited and trained as an armed militia:

> 'To compromise fascism in eyes of the petty-bourgeois and pave the way for the conquest of power by the proletariat.'
>
> - Leon Trotsky

On the question of war he opposed pacifism and argued that the only way to end war:

> '*Is the disarmament of the bourgeois by the workers. But to disarm the bourgeois the workers must first arm themselves.*'
>
> - Leon Trotsky

Finally Trotsky argued in the 'Transitional Programme' that members of the 4th International should concentrate on organizing the most exploited sections of the masses who are, he argued, women and the youth.

Victor Serge responded to the 4th International with venom accusing them of 'sectarianism' and 'engaging in intransigent polemics.' But because he didn't accept the programme of transitional demands he degenerated into a form of 'bureaucratic collectivism' arguing that a 'total bureaucratic society' was emerging and the only way ahead was a 'new minimum programme' for the masses. He died isolated and in dreadful poverty in Mexico and was buried in a paupers grave which only gained a headstone in 1992. His wife had descended into complete insanity years before. Serge had failed to win the debate with Trotsky and true to his first pseudonym 'Le Retif' (The Awkward Customer') refused to draw the correct conclusions.

The 4th International didn't see the aspirations invested in it by Trotsky achieve fruition but in a variety of manifestations it continues to exist. But how should revolutionaries understand it today, clearly it emanates from 60 odd years ago?. It is a mistake to see the 'Transitional Programme' as sacred text set in stone, but the methodology employed is still relevant today.

www.ingramcontent.com/pod-product-compliance
Lightning Source LLC
Chambersburg PA
CBHW031216270326
41931CB00006B/578